THE SOUL VOICE

A COLLECTION OF SHORT ENGLISH POEMS

SARAL

Made with ❤ on the Notion Press Platform
www.notionpress.com

Contents

Preface

Began with poetry writing since my childhood in Hindi language I wrote many short poems to recite them in my school cultural programme.

On each first Saturday of every month the school management organized Bal Sabha cultural programme.

Initially, Saturday programme fascinated me to write something differently.

The applauses and appreciations received from our friends, seniors and teachers were motivating factors for me.

Positive enforcements received from a quality human resource guided me for constant self writing upto 12th standard.

The appreciations and rewards gained in form of endless clappings and in teachers' responses in form of motivating remarks kept me insisting to write and present something newer and valuable.

Repeatedly, friends gave me a push to pen a new poem.

I did not let those opportunities in vain.

My writing this way grew instinctly.

Each time, I had something to ponder about.

Each time, I had something inside me to make me sit for a longer to put on the paper.

At the peak of my poetry writing I sacrificed my studies and meals at night to complete the pouring lines from the depth of my heart.

Each day, I had enough to write down without a pause.

Friends listened me in the programme.

Seniors made me the corrections.Teachers picked up me ahead in the classroom for studies and co -curricular activities on the priority basis.

My dedication for studies and writing made me always a disciplined student in the school.

At initial stage, my teachers recognized my potential and backed me always.

Their special attention guided me indirectly to follow the right path.

Far away from my hometown and parents I never felt alone under their care and affection.

Blessed with their compliments I never skipped my routine of writing and completing the assigned activities timely.

Days and days I got matured inside the premise of creative and effective environment of my Government school [Government Senior Secondary School For Blind Boys King's way Camp New Delhi] run under the department of social welfare.

As I mentioned earlier, initially, I began poetry writing in Hindi language.

Later, when I joined JNU for masters degree in ancient history I learnt academic writing skills in English language.

Here, I spent a lot of time in going through many books written in English language.

Gradually, learning developed effectively.

Concept and perception fermentation process took enough time.

This whole process of learning was coincided with my natural instinct of poetry writing.

It is said that sincerely done hard work and dedication put up for one's task returns a plenty for the time to come.

The same thing happened with me.

Several exercises done with words and lines helped me to articulate my emotions, feelings, experiences and responses into a poetic sense while began writing in English language coincidently.

I had never planned to write in English language. Fortunately, on a certain auspicious day I struck with this idea that I have a little bit sense of writing in English language.

And that holy and positive idea awakened me to pen down differently in English language.

Tougher circumstances faced at different stages; inclusion/exclusion, acceptance/rejection, love/hatred pleasure/sorrows confronted at certain moments of life culminated my feelings, emotions, experiences and hidden responses in the form of unseen flowing river inside my inner core of a sensible soul. And that wettened soul with abstract water kept me alive forever. This abstract extremely sensitive deep frozen water time-to-time as a cool and calm fountain pierced out of extra responsive soul.

And as a result, these hearty abstract fountains laid the foundation for short and simple poems. For a highly literary person there might be nothing to read about.

But, who is interested to stand with one's ongoing or previous struggles may explore enough between these poetic lines.

Hence, here, in this book the literary work is not done by a classical person but initiated by a lay person.

A person who has no literary experience of writing in English language.

Therefore, readers are expected to be a little bit polite while going through these poems. Try to sense the emotions and feelings that I have somehow tried to express out through these short poems.

Acknowledgements

Before, proceeding ahead inside the book I sincerely convey my hearty gratitudes to my teachers taught me at all levels.

I am deeply filled with great respect and devotion for those teachers who understood me and helped me to stand alone confidently by doing hard work.

I still feel their contribution whenever, I perform something valuable and qualitative in my life.

I recall my friends' efforts done for me to make me stronger.

They proved as a companion for me always.I use their contribution as a powerful tools. They still stay in my memories and enrich my experiences shared with them in the past.

I offer a humble salute to my father who stood with me as a strong pillar.

He taught me not to bow down if you find yourself on the right path.

How can I forget my wife's contribution.

She encouraged me to take different challenges.

She went through my writing and admired me critically.

Ending up I am greatly thankful to whole Notion Press Publication Team who judged this script as a fruitful content to publish. Without their humble guidance I could not move a single step.

Introduction

We and the world around us make a collage of different experiences which more or less beautify our life. We as a learner sometimes pleasantly enjoy these experiences since they appear to be fruitful according to our ambitions. Sometimes, we take them otherwise and indulge ourselves into a chaotic dismay. At one hand, these experiences may prove to someone inspiring to uprise one's morale. But, at reverse these may lead us to a destructive path of our moral and social degradation.Consequently,

both conditions of life formulate twofold worlds around us.

One is what we want to be and another is what we do not prove to be.

As a learner we do not take these incidents or conditions worthless. Instead we take them as motivating stimuli for our life. Experiences, harsh or loving always learn us a lesson.

And this lesson derived from our own experiences let us enlightened forever.

Abstract or non-abstract, visible or non-visible said or unsaid everything is important in the way of a long journey for our unstoppable steps.

Whatever, we have faced or conflicted with in this path of long journey does not go for a waste.

For an awared and awakened person everything that comes to take place proves an ingredient making his/her character more mature and stable despite having much tougher situations to confront with.

Humiliation, agony, prejudices, taboos, desperations, individual or racial discrimination etc give us a hault for a certain period of time but, later when our spirit pops up again and our inner voice gives us a push to renovate us we get renewed and revived everytime.

And thus, we repeatedly, indulge in a process of losing and gaining some virtues cementing our character more stronger and solidified.

Once, we start learning something fruitful throughout our present and past.

Once, we learn to accommodate ourselves in the situations we never hoped to confront with.

Once, we learn to respond positively we take a step ahead to mold the self.

Since my childhood I have learnt to sense the things deeply. My wisdom made me decisive in an unique way. I learnt to observe and respond patiently. And this way twofold character of mine helped to understand the self and mold the self in its wholeness.

My character that remained always disciplined and creative provided me the ground to support my creativity.

At parallel poetic sense inbuilt inside me instinctly opened a wider arena to perceive the world around me.

Curiosity to understand others behaviour and self judgmental power enabled me to form my individuality differently.

Earned characteristics, virtues and poetic abilities skilled me to be on the rumination for a longer time. It equipped me with a self regulating framework to pacify my mind and think for a while in a productive way.It made me more effectively trained to have a philosophical stand to come out of my jumbled thoughts and ignited my mind a little bit more positive and rational manner to mull over an idea.

The self constructed through a long process gave me the following lessons to orient myself on the way of spiritual development. And Firstly, I got lit with this notion that if new things do not take place for a long duration it would mark a negative impact on our surroundings.Secondly, it sharpened my intellect to think for that situation where nothing comes newer. Nothing takes place for a change. I think this situation would surely indulge us in the state of boredom. Our eyes desire to look something newer on each day. Our ears desire to listen something newer on each day. Our feet desire to walk on a newer path on each day. Overall, we love to embrace something newer on each day. It means that generating something newer is a philosophy of human life. If, we do not produce something newer we start reducing our value in our surroundings. As an idea producing something newer is an umbrella theory that includes many sub-theories enlarging our social and cultural graph. If, our heart is always open for embracing something newer we respect the change in the hours to come. We honour the culture of being renovating and innovating leaving the past behind full of mistakes or goodness in the days to come. We love the mutual coexistence of each other irrespective of having different ideological grounds shared in the past or awaited in the coming future.

Therefore, we should be hopeful for new morning to come. We should be hopeful for the time to come. We should be hopeful for the days to come. We should wait keenly for the gentle light of a new morning stayed a little bit away from our closed eyes in the night. What we have expected to be newer should come through a positive and gentle move with our compassionate heart respecting the mixed past and glorifying the future achievements with peace and calmness.

To conclude, I will say that my literary expressions are filled with mixed reactions to mold my identity and leave a constructive impact on external world that I confront with everyday.

Poem 1. I wish to be

I wish to walk

The ways filled with turns,

I wish to walk

The ways bring me no hate no thorns,

I wish to walk

The ways bring me new dreams new hopes,

I wish not to walk

The ways bring me deceit and mistrust.

I wish to walk

The gardens full of beauty,

I wish to walk

The gardens which governed by equity,

I wish to walk

The gardens bring me the sense of humanity,

I wish not to walk

Gardens trap me in the world of darkness.

I wish to sing

The songs of peace,

I wish to sing

The songs sound for no tease,

I wish to sing

The songs bring me the sense of calm and ease,

I wish not to sing

The songs full of hate and deceit.

I wish to talk

The people look simple and calm

I wish to talk

The people stand for no harm,

I wish to talk

SARAL

The people lead me the world of belief,

I wish not to talk

The people indulge me in a world of chaos.

Poem 2. The voice

Deep in my heart

The words of cry,

Deep in my heart

This gloom so high,

Deep in my heart

This pain and I,

No one knows I cry for why?

Each day I have

Lots of to say,

Each day I wish something to pray,

Each day I feel a constant decay,

No one knows what I want to say.

There are several

SARAL

People to talk,

There are people

Come with me to walk,

There are people

Leave on me a mark,

No one knows the secrets so dark.

Poem 3. I recall them

The days when I

Lived alone,

The days when I

Kept crying alone,

The days when I

Sighed in sorrow and pain,

Still I remember those days again.

The days when I

Faced struggle a lot,

The days when I

Meant for no thrill no joy,

The days when I

Felt left out always,

Still I respect those days again.

The days when I

Had no hands to hold,

The days when I

Had no hands to mold,

The days when I

Had no hands to make me the bold,

Still I enjoy those days again.

The days when I

Laughed on me

For no gain no success,

The days when I

Lacked continuity and pace,

The days when I

Sat years for no race,

Still I miss those days again.

The days when I

Had no books no pen,

The days when I

Had enough time to vain,

The days when I

Had a heart full of pain,

Still I celebrate those days again.

The days when I

Had no coins to eat,

The days when I

Had no one to meet,

The days when I

Had nothing to breathe,

Still I worship those days again.

The days those

Brought me will and patience,

SARAL

The days those

Taught me a lesson of silence,

The days those

Learnt me to swallow hate and annoyance,

I love forever those days to retain.

Poem 4. Should not repeat again

The things which made us

Full of anger

Should not repeat again,

The things which made us

Trapped into danger

Should not repeat again,

The things which made us

Full of sorrow

Should not repeat again.

The days which made us

Unkind and rude

Should not repeat again,

The days which made us

Cunning and shrewd

Should not repeat again,

The days which made us

Full of misery and impatience

Should not repeat again.

The men who led us

The path of unrest

Should not meet again,

The men who led us

The path of injustice

Should not meet again,

The men who led us

The path of violence

Should not meet again.

The phases those were

So barbaric and anarchic

Should not repeat again,

The phases those were

Known for no means

Should not repeat again,

The phases those

Prevailed for centuries for no cause

Should not repeat again.

The talks which made us

Full of confusions

Should not repeat again,

The talks which made us

Sane and ingenerous

Should not repeat again,

The talks which led us

For no solutions

Should not repeat again.

Poem 5. The all lost

The ways those

Used to walk for a journey

Lost away somewhere,

The ways those

Used to travel for millions of milestones

Lost away somewhere,

The ways those

Led us to the path of justice

Lost away somewhere.

The trees those

Grew up to touch the sky

Lost away somewhere,

The trees those

Grew up for fruits and medicine

Lost away somewhere,

The trees those

Grew up to produce life and prosperty

Lost away somewhere.

The flours those

Were used to smile for goodwill

Lost away somewhere,

The flours those

Blossomed for a new morning

Lost away somewhere,

The flours those

Were known for peace and gentleness

Lost away somewhere.

The birds those

Used to chirp in the morning

SARAL

Lost away somewhere,

The birds those

Sang for a melody

Lost away somewhere,

The birds those

Taught us to fly in the sky

Lost away somewhere.

The gentlemen those

Were so kind and generous

Lost away somewhere,

The gentlemen those

Stood up for justice and brotherhood

Lost away somewhere,

The gentlemen those

Enlightened the millions

Lost away somewhere.

Poem 6. The dark

Dark, dark dark,

Everything is dark.

The sky is dark

The earth is dark,

The night is dark

The day is dark,

Whatever you see

Looks dark and dark.

The men are dark

The soul is dark,

The minds are dark,

Whatever you act

Looks dark and dark.

SARAL

We are dark

You are dark,

Nothing to say all are dark,

What do we think

Everything proves dark and dark.

Our will is dark

Our swear is dark,

Each day we do

Our promise is dark,

Intentions inside us each day we make

None of them are pious

But dark and dark.

I lit the lamps to make the light

I have a will to see you the hight,

I pray to make the world so bright,

No one is willing to look into my eyes

Since, the minds of all manifest mere dark and dark.

Poem 7. The power inside us

The thing enacts in ups and downs,

The thing enacts us to bear pros and cons,

The thing enacts us to set milestones,

We don't know but only perceive it

The power inside us,

The power inside us.

The thing enacts us to step ahead,

The thing prevents us not to turn back,

The thing enacts us not to go fad,

We don't know but only we use it

The power inside us,

The power inside us.

When there would be

No one to stand aside us,

When there would be

Nothing to hide us,

When there would be

No one to coincide us,

We will rejoice we will retain

The power inside us,

The power inside us.

When there would be

A millions of hurdles,

When we would be

Trapped into the the troubles,

When we would be

Bound into the circles,

Even we would be having to claim

The power inside us,

SARAL

The power inside us.

Poem 8. I need to

I need to

Spend a while of calm,

I need to

Spend a while of charm,

I need to

Spend a while with no harm,

I do not need to

Extend a fragile and alarm.

I need to

Look at the beauty that's divine,

I need to

Look at the beauty that's mine,

I need to

Look at the beauty that brings me the shine,

I do not need to

Look at what brings me a ruin.

I need to

Sing a song of peace,

I need to

Sing a song of relief,

I need to

Sing a song full of ease,

I do not need to

Sing a song full of hate and tease.

Poem 9. Your lovely smile

When the gloom

Haunts me alone,

When my heart is full of mourn,

When I feel

A danger unknown,

I do recall

Your lovely smile.

When the eyes

Go red in anger,

When the heart

Beats faster and longer,

When a friend

Turns into a stranger,

SARAL

I hope for a glance

Your lovely smile.

When I face

The world unkind,

When I find an unrest in my mind,

When I wish something

Not to remind,

I only coincide

Your lovely smile.

When the flowers

Bloom for untold beauty,

When the trees

Swing for bringing the equity,

When the air

Blows spreading the sense of liberty,

I am always echoed

With your lovely smile.

Poem 10. The beauty of sleep

The noisy days

Bring us unrest,

The body and the soul

Want peaceful rest,

The talks and gossips day around,

Lead us the way that's only for waste,.

Far away from day and chaos,

Night awaits for a wonderful world.

The days pass by at a pace,

We get trapped find no space,

The feet go weary,

The soul goes down,

We get worthy nothing to chase,

The night awaited brings us the hope

We will having a sigh of relief.

Ahead a hasty speedy time,

Ahead a dizzy task that was assigned,

Ahead the quarrels that we engage,

Ahead the unkind heapy outrage.

The sleep awaited wrapped in the dreams

Let us enjoy a beautiful spring.

The sleepy grasses cool and calm,

The downward branches with secrets in their palm,

The snowy mountains up in the sky,

Stand alone with beauty and charm.

The sleep awaited let them all

The world of beauty with silence and calm.

The sleepy rivers with gentle flow,

The wind with love blows calm and slow,

SARAL

Have a touch them lovely to know.

The sleeping world with unsaid beauty

Says nothing has lots of to show.

Poem 11. Should we?

Where there the ways are blocked,

Where there we always are stopped,

Where there all doors are locked,

Should we proceed on that way.

Where there we get ignored,

Where there we always get mourned,

Where there we get insecured,

Should we like that place to stay.

Where there our words get useless,

Where there we get always hopeless,

Where there we get always restless,

Should we like that place to praise.

Where there our face goes fad,

Where there our eyes go red,

Where there we go for mad,

Should we love those people to embrace.

Poem 12. We are the same

Let us stay for a while,

Let us play for while,

We are children not as you are

Let us walk on the same way for a while,

Why do you divide when we are the same.

Let us sit for a hearty laughter,

Let us meet on a lovely matter,

Let us forget the hharshiest matter,

Why do you provoke when we are the same.

Let us unite to live with peace,

Let us unite to live with ease,

We want not to quarrel a more,

Let us unite for bridging up the gapes,

Why do you lit a fire among us

When we are the same.

• 33 •

Poem 13. The Soul Cries

When I listen

Someone teasing to a kind man,

When I listen

Someone abusing to a gentle man,

When I listen

Someone vanishing generosity gentleness and purety in vain

The soul of gentle men

Full with sorrow,

Hurts and cries.

When I see

A peaceful mind perturbed,

When I see

A man so caring and loving disturbed,

SARAL

When I see

A man so soft and calm

Gets always trapped and troubled.

The heart of mine goes down and I

Let me a while

In the world of sighs.

When I listen

The roaring voices,

When I listen

Needless taunts so harsh,

When I listen

Someone's goodness remains unheard,

I come to know

The sin and the sinners

Are on the rise.

Poem 14. Enlighten yourself

Hands with you

Touch and sense

Why do you perceive the things

Those are not here.

Feet with you

Walk and see

Why do you believe

The world that illusioned

For you to deceive.

Eyes with you

Look and wathch

Why are you trapped

Into the false world

That's always unheard and unseen.

Your intellect with you

Think and decide

Why do you trust someone else

Who is not for you and not with you.

Who loves you

Surely will come to embrace,

Who loves you

Surely will come to raise,

Who loves you

Surely will come to praise,

Who loves you

Surely will give you the courage

Why do you excite your soul for them

Who never stood to guard your dignity and privilege.

Poem 15. Morning delays

Night seems not to come at end,

It only takes the steps to extend.

Slept men will never get a chance for a rise,

Never they will see a sun rise.

Concious years will desperatlely wait for a chirping sound,

Never they will never be able to enjoy that sound.

Eyes will desperately wait for a look of swinging trees,

Never they will never find aglance as they would go freeze.

We'll desperately wait for lovely words,

Never we'll never meet such fortune to exchange our hearty words.

Hands will desperately wait for a friendly shake,

Never we'll never be so friendly to offer a healthy handshake.